CRABAPPL

"Look, there's a fox,"
seen us."
"Look how fast it can run," said Claire.
The fox disappeared into the wood.
"It wasn't us who frightened the fox, look over there," laughed Jim.

Over a low fence came old
farmer Gumboot.
"Over we go me beauty!" he cried, then
almost fell off.
He patted his horse, waved to Claire
and rode on.
"Hello Mr Gumboot," shouted Claire and
she waved back.
"Hello!" shouted Mr Gumboot as he
disappeared over another fence.

Claire and Jim continued to walk through the fields and the wood.
"It's getting late, we had better go home," said Jim.
"What's that man doing over there?" asked Claire.
Jim didn't know.
"What are you doing?" he shouted.

"We're going to build houses here," said the man, "we're going to cut down the wood and build lots of nice houses, some shops and perhaps a cinema. You'd like that wouldn't you?"

Claire and Jim ran home and told Mum and Dad about the man and what he had said.

"They can't do that," said Mum, "they can try but we won't let them".

"Will you write something in your newspaper Dad?" asked Claire. "Tell them they can't cut down the wood."

"I'll do what I can," said Dad.
"Perhaps when everyone hears about the wood they will stop the developers cutting down the trees."
"Make it good Dad," said Jim.
"How could farmer Gumboot sell his land to a developer?" said Claire.

Daily News

Crabapple Wood to be cut down.

Rumours that Crabapple Wood is to be cut down for a housing estate have made local people very angry. They say they will fight to save the wood from the developer, Mr Vulture.

Claire and Jim visited the wood nearly every day. They saw men in big cars and smart suits come to look at the wood. Then one day a man with a chain saw arrived. They had to do something to stop him cutting down the trees.

They watched as the forester put down his saw and got out his sandwiches and a bottle of drink.
"Hello," said Claire, "what a lovely day for a picnic."
The man said he was not having a picnic, he was here to cut down trees.

Jim and Claire pretended to look worried.
"How awful, let's get away before he starts," said Claire, and they started to hurry away.
"Wait, what do you mean by, 'how awful'?" said the man.
"Didn't they tell you? They should have told you," said Claire, "about the curse."

The man looked worried.
" 'The curse', what do you mean,
'the curse'?"
"The curse on whoever cuts down the trees,
oh it's too awful to talk about," said
Claire, and they ran off.
The man stood for some time just looking
into the wood, then he drove away.
Claire and Jim ran all the way to see
their Dad in the newspaper office.

J.G. was working in his office when
Claire and Jim rushed in. They told him
about the man with the chain saw
and how Claire had made up a story
about a curse. J.G. thought it was
a lovely story.
"The curse of Crabapple Wood, I like it,"
said J.G.
"What a clever daughter I've got!"
And they all laughed.

Daily News

The Crabapple Wood curse.

There has always been a Crabapple Wood and if the Crabapple curse is true, there will always be one. For hundreds of years, those who were stupid enough to cut down trees in the wood have had awful things happen to them.

The man with the saw went to see Mr Vulture in his office.

"I'm not cutting your trees down," he said, "the curse may not be true but I'm not taking a chance".

"Then I'll get someone who will," said Mr Vulture.

So he put an advert in J.G.'s newspaper.

Forester required by Developers.

Forester required to cut down trees in Crabapple Wood. Good pay. Apply at once to Vultures Ltd. 'Phone 07191263.

Next to the advert J.G. wrote:

Local curse.
True or false?

Local people believe the curse on anyone cutting down trees in Crabapple Wood should be taken seriously. They say the curse goes back hundreds of years and something awful has happened to all those who have ignored the warning.

Of course no-one answered the advert. No-one wanted to take the chance of something awful happening to them. Mr Vulture got very cross,
"What's the matter with everyone?" he said.
"If I can't get someone to cut down the trees, I'll cut them down myself."

J.G. found out when Mr Vulture planned to start his tree cutting, and told people when this was in the newspaper. When Mr Vulture arrived with his chain saw there were lots of people in his way.
"I'll try again tomorrow and I'll have a policeman with me," he said.

The next day the policeman came to Crabapple Wood and made everyone get out of the way. They could only watch as Mr Vulture picked up his chain saw. Then it began to rain and as he tried to start the saw the rain got heavier. But the saw wouldn't start and he got very angry.

He tried extra hard to start the saw, slipped and fell into a puddle. Everyone laughed and cheered but then something awful happened. They had all cheered just as farmer Gumboot was jumping the fence. The noise frightened the horse and the farmer fell off.

Poor old Mr Gumboot was dead when they picked him up. Everyone was very upset and they began to move away to go home. Then Mr Vulture called out, "It's the curse, it's true! Someone is dead and we haven't even started yet."
The people around him agreed, and he put the chain saw into his car and drove away.

Claire tried to tell the people the story of the curse was not true, that she had made it up. But they wouldn't believe her. J.G. put his arm round his daughter's shoulder, "They won't believe you," he said.
Then he went back to the newspaper office to write his story of what had happened.

Daily News

Farmer who sold Wood dies in protest.

Mr Gumboot, who was much loved by everyone, died after falling from his horse in Crabapple Wood. Mr Vulture, the developer, was very upset by his death and has decided not to continue with his plan to cut down the wood.

Some weeks later Claire and Jim were walking through the wood.
"People won't come into the wood anymore, they think it's haunted," said Jim.
"How stupid," said Claire, "I don't believe in ghosts."
Then they distinctly heard: "Over we go me beauty," and the sound of a galloping horse.